*W*hen a Man Loves a Walnut

and Even More Misheard Lyrics

By Gavin Edwards

Illustrated by Shary Flenniken

A Fireside Book · Published by Simon & Schuster

Fireside
Rockefeller Center
1230 Avenue of the Americas
New York, NY 10020

Designed by Bonni Leon-Berman

Manufactured in the United States of America

1   3   5   7   9   10   8   6   4   2

Library of Congress Cataloging-in-Publication Data is available

ISBN 0-684-84567-9

This book is dedicated to the memory of Renée Crist Sheffield, fount of music, laughter, and love.

Introduction

You may not know the word *mondegreen*—it's only a little over forty years old, coined by Sylvia Wright in a 1954 *Atlantic* article. But you certainly know the phenomenon: it was that time a Beatles song came on the radio, and you sang along with them. Only *you* were belting out "she's got a tick in her eye" instead of "she's got a ticket to ride."

This phenomenon seems to happen in the world of musical lyrics more often than anyplace else—that's why this book is the third volume in a series, following *'Scuse Me While I Kiss This Guy and Other Misheard Lyrics* and *He's Got the Whole World in His Pants and More Misheard Lyrics.* (Collect 'em all! No scholarly mondegreen library—or bathroom— is complete without the whole set.) One reason is the tendency of many singers to mumble rather than articulate. This may be out of laziness, a desire to appear cryptic, or a frantic effort to obscure banal lyrics.

The other reason, of course, lies with the listeners: We've learned not to pay much attention to the lyrics of rock or pop songs, but rather to let them wash over us so we can pick out individual phrases and choruses that we enjoy. (Some bands, like Pavement and the Fall, take advantage of our inconsistent ears and write bitter, gnarled verses in what seem to be cheerful pop songs.) Some people never learn the words to a favorite song—or transmute them into something more to their own taste. My friend Alma liked Billy Idol's "Eyes Without a Face" *because* she thought the title was "I Supply the Fish." To my mind, this is a good thing, and not just because it lets me put out these collections of mondegreens. Pop songs aren't Ph.D. dissertations or instruction manuals: They're *supposed* to be heard a million different ways, in a million different contexts. Customization is the only rational response to omnipresence.

So people continue to mangle lyrics and send me mondegreens by the bushel, either boldly owning up to their errors or cravenly blaming close friends and relatives for the mistakes. I make every human effort to separate the deliberate mishearings from those of the confused and befuddled; some of the most humiliating mistakes come from the most earnest sources. Misheard lyrics often become family legends, as evidenced by this letter from Daniel Brotschul of Gainesville, Florida: "I'll never forget singing 'Paperlate' by Genesis while in the shower as an elementary school student. I thought it was 'Paper Lake.' When I got out of the shower, I was humiliated by my siblings, who mocked me, saying, 'Look! You're all wet! You've got confetti in your hair! Anyone want to go for a swim in Lake Memo?' "

Some folks get so confused by the lack of articulation in the musical world that they begin to mangle *band names,* calling Hüsker Dü the inappropriate "Who Skidoo." This is why people mistakenly refer to Andy

Gibb as "Auntie Gibb," Hall and Oates as "Hollow Notes," and Sam and Dave as "Salmon Dave." It doesn't, however, explain those few who refer to Bruce Springsteen as "The Chief" rather than "The Boss."

Some readers may recall that in the last volume of this series, *He's Got the Whole World in His Pants and More Misheard Lyrics,* I inducted the first slate of members into the Misheard Lyrics Hall of Fame: John Fogerty, Mick Jagger, Elton John, Steve Miller, Michael Stipe, and Eddie Vedder. For their exemplary work in slurring vowels *and* consonants, and their role in providing an endless supply of mondegreens, I am honored to name the second group of inductees: Kurt Cobain, Bob Dylan, Jack Ely (lead singer on the Kingsmen's "Louie Louie"), Chrissie Hynde, Stevie Nicks, and Gavin Rossdale.

Rossdale, the lead singer of Bush, has provoked so many diverse mishearings in the past few years, you could compile completely erroneous versions of his songs by merging the errors of his fans. So that's what I've done with Bush's first hit, "Everything Zen." First, the correct lyrics:

> *There must be something we can eat*
> *Maybe find another lover*
> *Should I fly to Los Angeles*
> *Find my asshole brother*
>
> *Mickey Mouse has grown up a cow*
> *Dave's on sale again*
> *We kissy kiss in the rear view*

We're so bored
You're to blame

Try to see it once my way
Everything zen
Everything zen
I don't think so

Raindogs howl for the century
A million dollars a steak
As you search for your demi-god
And you fake with a saint
There's no sex in your violence
There's no sex in your violence

Try to see it once my way
Everything zen
Everything zen
I don't think so

I don't believe that Elvis is dead
I don't believe that Elvis is dead
I don't believe that Elvis is, Elvis is

There's no sex in your violence

x

Granted, not every lyric in the song makes literal sense, but it's not too hard to determine the general intention: a sketch of America at the millenium, with the singer in awe at all the cultural excess. Now, consider the way of our errors:

There must be someone with weed
Maiden finds another lover
Should I fly horizontally
Find my asshole, brother?

Hakeem now has gone kapow!
The days all sound like sand
Kids eat kids and the real you
You're a whore
You're too lame

Trashy was my wife
Everything zen
Everything zen
I don't think so

Graveyards howl for the sins you eat
A million dollars at stake
You search for your demi-bra
And your fake feather cape

There's no sex in your violins
There's no sex in New Orleans

Squashy was my wine
A workman's end
A workman's end
I don't think so

I don't believe it ever since then
I don't believe that Alice is dead
I don't believe in elephants' innocence

There's no sex in your violets
There's no sex in Hawaii
There's no sex in Ohio
There's no sex in Rhode Island

Does this version make more sense? Can you deny the power of its accidental poetry? I don't think so.

Here's how the rest of the mondegreens in *When a Man Loves a Walnut* are organized:

Wrong lyric

Artist

Song title

Right lyric

In cases where there's more than one misheard version of the same line, here's how we print them:

- First wrong lyric
- Second wrong lyric

Artist

Song title

Right lyric

Scrubbing my bear with his fingers

The Fugees
"Killing Me Softly" 4:46

Strumming my fate with his fingers

When a man loves a walnut

Percy Sledge

"When a Man Loves a Woman" 2:50

When a man loves a woman

Tea leaves, they can't ski on a legal holiday

Pearl Jam

"Even Flow"

Ceilings, few and far between all the legal halls of shame

Water, water, water's free

The Beatles
"Come Together" 4:16

One and one and one is three

I don't mind stealing bread from the mouths of elephants

Temple of the Dog

"Hunger Strike" 4:07

I don't mind stealing bread from the mouths of decadence

A wiener wrap, a wiener wrap

The Tokens
"The Lion Sleeps Tonight" 2:35

A wimoweh, a wimoweh

Making love to his tonic engine

Billy Joel
"Piano Man" 5:33

Making love to his tonic and gin

Just another mad podiatrist

Bob Marley and the Wailers

"Exodus"

Come on people, let me tell you this

- It's just no good / The cheese in life tastes better
- It's just no good / You're teasing like a whore
- It's just no good / Your cheese is life in Denver

Blondie

"Heart of Glass"

It's just no good / You're cheating like you do

Maybe I'm just like my father—too bald

Prince

"When Doves Cry" 5:52

Maybe I'm just like my father—2 bold

I'm gonna braid a rustic Cajun rug

Soundgarden

"Rusty Cage"

I'm gonna break my rusty cage and run

Showing the zebra love

Tears for Fears

"Sowing the Seeds of Love" 6:16

Sowing the seeds of love

Little G-Man

Elton John
"Little Jeannie" 5:11

Little Jeannie

Cows and people in the street

Buffalo Springfield
"For What It's Worth" 2:38

A thousand people in the street

You're the king with the dog nose

Hanson

"MMMBop"   4:16

You say you can't, but you don't know

Keep your eyes on the road 'til your hands break down in Rio

The Doors

"Roadhouse Blues"   4:00

Keep your eyes on the road, your hands upon the wheel

You got a rat for a mama, Sherry baby

The Four Seasons
"Sherry Baby" 2:45

You better ask your mama, Sherry baby

That deft thumb of lightning

The Who
"Pinball Wizard" 3:00

That deaf, dumb, and blind kid

14

No, I can't forget the semen on your face as you were leaving

---

Mariah Carey
"Without You"   3:38

No, I can't forget this evening / Or your face as you were leaving

I am the worrier

Scandal featuring Patty Smyth
"The Warrior"   3:47

I am the warrior

Batman watergun

Bush

"Glycerine"

Bad moon wine again

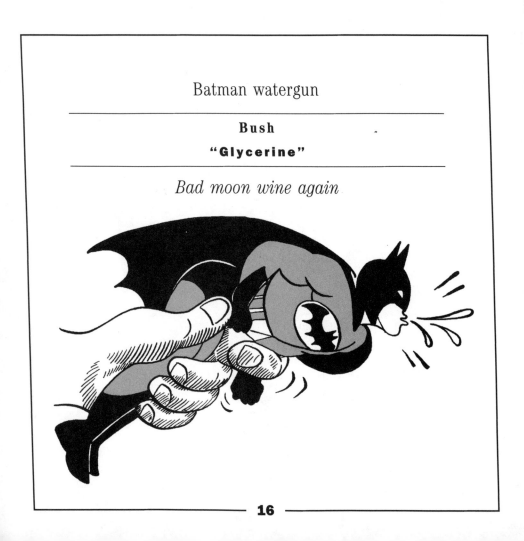

Everybody plays the flute sometimes

The Main Ingredient
"Everybody Plays the Fool" 3:28

Everybody plays the fool sometimes

I wish they offered me California girls

The Beach Boys
"California Girls" 2:38

I wish they all could be California girls

- Spied on my radio, still just a rat in a cage
- The spider marines, Siam's steel-chested rabbit arcade

Smashing Pumpkins
"Bullet with Butterfly Wings" 4:14

In spite of my rage, I am still just a rat in a cage

Shit!

Paul McCartney and Wings
"Jet" 4:07

Jet!

Oh Mandy, you kissed me and stopped me from shaving

Barry Manilow

"Mandy" 3:15

Oh Mandy, you kissed me and stopped me from shaking

I want a new truck

Huey Lewis and the News
"I Want a New Drug" 4:47

I want a new drug

My mere bits of shame

The Andrews Sisters

"Bei Mir Bist Du Schoen"

Bei mir bist du schoen

Are you disrespecting me? Drink your milk—you got to keep 'em separated

---

The Offspring

"Come Out and Play" 3:05

. . . take 'em out—you got to keep 'em separated

- Rocket man, burning up the trees on every lawn
- Rocket man, turning out his shoes for everyone
- Rocket man, burning up the tarp forever more

Elton John

"Rocket Man" 4:42

Rocket man, burning out his fuse up here alone

But if you go carrying pictures of German mouths

The Beatles
"Revolution" 3:24

But if you go carrying pictures of Chairman Mao

I am a sphincter / I'm the real thing

R.E.M.
"Crush with Eyeliner" 4:35

I am smitten / I'm the real thing

Skinny, skinny, skinny's getting heavy

Snap!
"The Power" 5:42

It's getting, it's getting, it's getting kinda hectic

I can't fight the ceiling any more

REO Speedwagon
"Can't Fight This Feeling" 4:54

I can't fight this feeling any more

Cheese corn

Hall and Oates

"She's Gone" 5:15

She's gone

Found Geronimo's rifle, Paris in shambles, and
anything that's closer to men

Sheryl Crow

"If It Makes You Happy" 5:23

---

*Found Geronimo's rifle, Marilyn's shampoo, and
Benny Goodman's corset and pen*

Don't want to be your funky friend

The Foo Fighters
"Monkey Wrench"

Don't want to be your monkey wrench

Don't bring me down, Bruce

Electric Light Orchestra
"Don't Bring Me Down"

Don't bring me down—grroosss

The cab drivers know us and they leave us alone

The Beach Boys
"I Get Around" 2:12

The bad guys know us and they leave us alone

- See the comb I bought
- I live on your block

Oye Como Va

Every day I get confused

The Who
"Magic Bus" *3:18*

Every day I get in the queue

You probably think this song is about you / Don't
shoot! Don't shoot!

Carly Simon
"You're So Vain" *4:15*

. . . . don't you, don't you?

- Simian girl
- Synonym girl

Neil Young

"Cinnamon Girl"   3:00

Cinnamon girl

Living, loving, she's just a walrus

Led Zeppelin

"Living Loving Maid (She's Just a Woman)"

Living, loving, she's just a woman

She must lead a very dull life, with just a cat on a hook by her side

---

Jill Sobule

"Karen by Night"

. . . with just a cat and a book by her side

She paints my chicken when I sleep

The Grateful Dead
"Sugar Magnolia" *3:15*

She pays my ticket when I speed

I want you to know / I'm half-baked for you

Alanis Morissette

"You Oughta Know"

I want you to know / I'm happy for you

Don't give us none of your aggravation / I had to make a touchdown pass

---

Elton John

"Saturday Night's Alright for Fighting"

Don't give us none of your aggravation / We've had it with your discipline

I wanna share my love with a woman lover

Donna Summer
"Bad Girls"

4:56

I wanna share my love with a warmer lover

Love me like a bum

Def Leppard

"Pour Some Sugar on Me" 4:25

Love me like a bomb

Yeah, just sitting back, dying of cancer

Bruce Springsteen

"Glory Days" 4:14

Yeah, just sitting back, trying to recapture

Are you really in the yeast? Stowin' away the tiles? /
Are you gatherin' up the teats? Have you had
enough of mime?

Steely Dan

"Reelin' in the Years" 4:35

---

*Are you reelin' in the years? Stowin' away the time? /
Are you gatherin' up the tears? Have you had
enough of mine?*

Throw down your American noose, so Ike can climb right back

Nirvana

"Heart-Shaped Box"

Throw down your umbilical noose, so I can climb right back

My mind is bacon, but my body's Sizzlean

Foreigner

"Double Vision"   3:43

My mind is racin', but my body's in the lead

Trouble in the sewers

Billy Joel

"We Didn't Start the Fire"

Trouble in the Suez

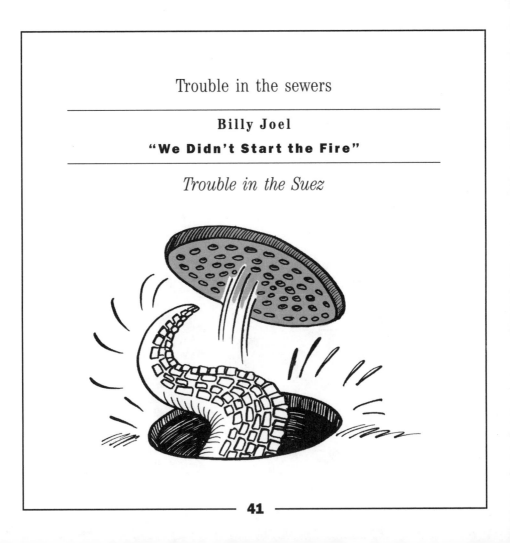

Put it in your pants, you're with your cupcake

Simon and Garfunkel

"Mrs. Robinson"

Put it in your pantry with your cupcakes

I used a decent, little boy

Smashing Pumpkins 3:13

"Disarm"

I used to be a little boy

Eagle chips is not my thing / All this strange waste
in chips really gets me down

Bobby Brown

"My Prerogative"

---

*Ego trips is not my thing / All these strange
relationships really get me down*

The way I feel about the Orkin man

10,000 Maniacs
"Because the Night" 3:46

The way I feel under your command

Foyer love

The Yardbirds
"For Your Love" 2:45

For your love

I want to act short

Alicia Bridges
"I Love the Nightlife (Disco Round)" 5:34

I want some action

To be bowling naked at your side

George Michael

"Father Figure"

To be bold and naked at your side

- Somebody's hiding a clown in my icebox
- Somebody's hiney is drowning my baseballs

Weezer

"Say It Ain't So" 4:11

Somebody's Heinie is crowding my icebox

Commie

Blondie
"Call Me"   *7:58*

Call me

You are on expeditions up the Amazon, uh-huh

R.E.M.

"What's the Frequency, Kenneth?"

You wore our expectations like an armored suit,
uh-huh

Cold coffee for change / Did you exchange a walk-on part in *The Wall* for a leaf rolled in a cave?

Pink Floyd
"Wish You Were Here" 4:43

Cold comfort for change / Did you exchange a walk-on part in the war for a leading role in a cage?

I saw the sun

Ace of Base
"The Sign" 3:21

I saw the sign

Wasting away in my gorilla suit

Jimmy Buffett
"Margaritaville"

Wasting away in Margaritaville

I don't care too much for Mommy / Mommy, can't Bobbi love?

The Beatles

"Can't Buy Me Love" 2:12

I don't care too much for money / Money can't buy me love

Who brought stripes and fried stars through the barrel of Sprite

---

Traditional

"The Star-Spangled Banner"

Whose broad stripes and bright stars through the perilous fight

I am still living with your goats

I am still living with your ghost

- Until the sun comes up I'll settle for a cupful of art
- Until the sun comes up on a cinnamon cup at the bar
- Until the sun comes up on a sentimental cup full of lard

Sheryl Crow

"All I Wanna Do"

Until the sun comes up over Santa Monica Boulevard

Strain my dick

Electric Light Orchestra
"Strange Magic" *3:53*

Strange magic

She stirs her ass in a glass with her L.A. gun finger

John Mellencamp
"Key West Intermezzo" *5:04*

She stirs her ice in a glass with her elegant finger

Strangers in the night, exchanging glasses

Frank Sinatra

"Strangers in the Night" 2:38

Strangers in the night, exchanging glances

Silk is now a food / Well, the change is news

Nirvana

"In Bloom"

Sell the kids for food / Weather changes moods

Killing me softly with insults

The Fugees
"Killing Me Softly"

Killing me softly with his song

I'm a girl

Elton John
"Island Girl" 3:46

Island girl

I've got a friend in cheese sauce

Norman Greenbaum
"Spirit in the Sky" 4:00

I've got a friend in Jesus

Fried trout! Uh-huh, bass, bass, bass

Peter Wolf

"Lights Out"

Lights out! Uh-huh, blast, blast, blast

There's a croissant, that is you

Sade

"Sweetest Taboo" 4:16

There's a quiet storm, that is you

It's all your fault / I scream my balls off

No Doubt

"Spiderwebs"   4:14

It's all your fault / I screen my phone calls

Slap that midget and then we'll go

The Beastie Boys

"Shadrach"

Shadrach, Meschach, Abednego

I got my flower, I got my power / I got a Roman nose

Led Zeppelin

"Dancing Days" 3:43

I got my flower, I got my power / I got a woman who knows

The price of beans, it's bringing me to my knees /
The beans! The price!

Def Leppard

"Love Bites" 5:46

---

*Love bites, love bleeds, it's bringing me to my
knees / Love bleeds, love bites*

Swedish in Haifa

Creedence Clearwater Revival
"Sweet Hitchhiker" 3:00

Sweet hitchhiker

Anal angel gonna greet me

Bruce Springsteen
"Streets of Philadelphia" 3:38

Ain't no angel gonna greet me

The clowns never expect it when it rains

Stevie Nicks

"Edge of Seventeen"

The clouds never expect it when it rains

I really don't agree with you

Hootie and the Blowfish

"Only Wanna Be With You" 3:46

I only wanna be with you

I saw the woman wearing the TV set

Duran Duran

"The Reflex" 5:27

I sold the Renoir and the TV set

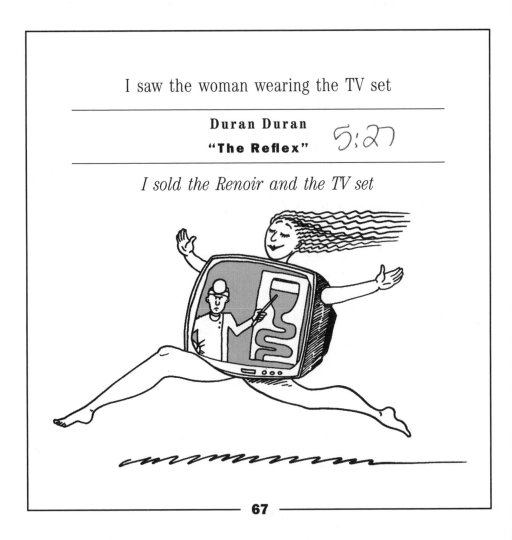

War is all around us / My mom and sis prepare to
fight

Prince

"1999" 6:16

. . . *My mind says prepare 2 fight*

Going to the jack-o'-lantern, gonna get married

The Dixie Cups

"Chapel of Love" *2:45*

Going to the chapel, and we're gonna get married

See the phone twist in your side

U2
"With or Without You" *21:58*

See the thorn twist in your side

Ah, shut your mouth, my wiggly spoon

Bush
"Little Things" *4:29*

I touch your mouth / My willy is food

Back to the heart attack tower

Elton John

"Goodbye Yellow Brick Road"

Back to the horny-back toad

Saturday night's alright for fighting / Better than election year

---

Elton John

"Saturday Night's Alright for Fighting"

Saturday night's alright for fighting / Get a little action in

I even like steak on a stack of knives

Elton John

"The Bitch Is Back" 3:42

I even like steak on a Saturday night

Just another man, it's Monday

The Bangles
"Manic Monday" *3:09*

Just another manic Monday

- There's a rose and a fist of blood
- There's a road in the distance, love

Stephen Stills
"Love the One You're With" *3:17*

There's a rose in the fisted glove

Lick the dirt off Olajuwon's feet

Pearl Jam

"Rats"

Lick the dirt off a larger one's feet

Edith was troubled by a horrible ass

R.E.M.

"Man on the Moon"

Egypt was troubled by the horrible asp

It's a girl, my Lord / In some fathead's Ford

The Eagles

"Take It Easy"

. . . in a flat-bed Ford

I'd rather be your circumflex

The Foo Fighters

"Monkey Wrench"

I'd rather leave than suffer this

Change yourself around real soon, make us
swimmin' in bed

John Cougar

"Jack and Diane" 4:16

---

*Changes come around real soon, make us women
and men*

Stain that skirt you've been hiding behind

Billy Joel
"Only the Good Die Young"

---

*The stained-glass curtain you've been hiding
behind*

I won't / Can he?

Bow Wow Wow
"I Want Candy" 2:45

I want candy

Turn the heater on

Vickie Sue Robinson
"Turn the Beat Around" 4:14

Turn the beat around

I know the birds and the bees

Alanis Morissette

"You Oughta Know"

An older version of me

I love you like Walter

Live
"All Over You"

Our love is like water

Obscene fire and obscene rain

James Taylor   3:14
"Fire and Rain"

I've seen fire and I've seen rain

Here come the Jetsons—one, two, three

Bad Company

"Rock and Roll Fantasy" 3:32

Here come the jesters—one, two, three

You can have my insulation, you can have the heat
that it brings / You can have my asbestos flakes

Nine Inch Nails

"Closer"

---

*You can have my isolation, you can have the hate
that it brings / You can have my absence of faith*

Eyelids in the street

Kenny Rogers with Dolly Parton
"Islands in the Stream" 4:08

Islands in the stream

- She's a bottom mover
- Cheetah bought a muu-muu

Sir Douglas Quintet
"She's About a Mover" 2:25

She's about a mover

Precious spacious nest of mangoes

David Bowie
"Moonage Daydream" 4:38

Press your space-face close to mine, love

Cheese and flies superstar

Murray Head 4:21

"Superstar—Jesus Christ Superstar"

Jesus Christ superstar

Looking for a sailor in these dirty streams /
Looking for a satyr beneath these dirty sheep

Tori Amos

"Crucify"

Looking for a savior in these dirty streets /
Looking for a savior beneath these dirty sheets

Carry a laser on the road that I must travel

Mr. Mister
"Kyrie"   4:14

Kyrie eleison on the road that I must travel

Everybody in the wholesale block

Elvis Presley
"Jailhouse Rock"   2:15

Everybody in the whole cellblock

Since you put me down, there's been owls puking
in my bed

The Beach Boys

"Help Me, Rhonda" 2:45

---

*Since she put me down, I been all through it in
my head*

Oh, say, does the star-sprinkled banana yet wave?

Traditional

"The Star-Spangled Banner"

O say, does that star-spangled banner yet wave?

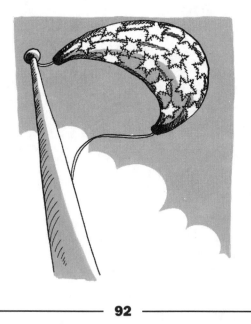

Go, go, Jason Waterfalls

TLC
"Waterfalls" 4:26

Don't go chasin' waterfalls

Thought of giving it all away / Too rich to share
the tea

Paul McCartney and Wings
"Band on the Run" 5:10

---

*Thought of giving it all away to a registered
charity*

Warm head lice

The Wallflowers
"One Headlight" 5:11

One headlight

For a pocketful of jumbo eggs and promises

Simon and Garfunkel
"The Boxer"

For a pocketful of mumbles, such are promises

Potty all the time

Eddie Murphy

"Party All the Time" 3:58

Party all the time

I need a lover, pork chops and gravy

Pat Benatar

"I Need a Lover"

I need a lover who won't drive me crazy

Sam and Janet evening

Ezio Pinza

"Some Enchanted Evening"

Some enchanted evening

- Requesting quiet
- Big Boston choir

10cc

"I'm Not in Love"

Big boys don't cry

And when I go, I want a lump of poop in my eye

Martin Page 4:42

"In the House of Stone and Light"

And when I go, I will op-op-open my eyes

My father is gonna hurt me

Weezer

"Why Bother"

Why bother / It's gonna hurt me

Virgin, virgin, emergency

Foreigner 4:29
"Urgent"

Urgent, urgent, emergency

She wears bad plaid pajamas

Carl Carlton

"She's a Bad Mama Jama (She's Built, She's Stacked)"

She's a bad mama jama

Gee, olive oil on salad's great

Archie and Edith Bunker
(Carroll O'Connor and Jean Stapleton)

"Those Were the Days (Theme from
***All in the Family*)"**

Gee, our old LaSalle ran great

Don't cry for me, Urgent Tina

Madonna 4:43

"Don't Cry for Me, Argentina"

Don't cry for me, Argentina

I watched the gleam as kings and queens fought
for tender cakes for the gods they'd made

The Rolling Stones

"Sympathy for the Devil" 6:19

I watched with glee while your kings and queens
fought for ten decades for the gods they'd made

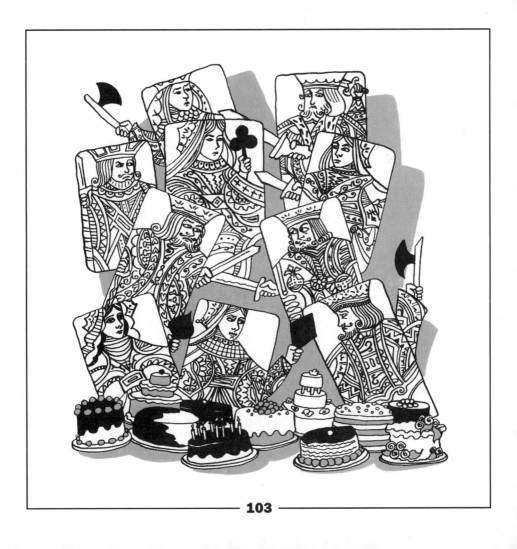

Looking for a class on Jung

The Beatles
"Glass Onion" 2:18

Looking through a glass onion

Hold on, Bruce Lee, and don't let go

.38 Special
"Hold on Loosely" 4:30

Hold on loosely and don't let go

If we sit on Marianne, what will we weigh?

Boston
"More Than a Feeling" *4:43*

I see my Marianne walkin' away

Sodomy is such a part of you

Smashing Pumpkins
"Disarm"

Inside of me and such a part of you

When the frills are right, I'm gonna sew all night

Bryan Adams
"Run to You" 3:46

When the feeling's right, I'm gonna run all night

Living on a fish island

Living in a fisheye lens

Is it any wonder I reject your breasts?

David Bowie

"Fame"

Is it any wonder I reject you first?

- Stamp Act
- Tampax

Stevie Nicks
"Stand Back" 4:53

Stand back

Deep within each heart, there lies a magic sock

Celine Dion

"The Power of the Dream"

. . . there lies a magic spark

Ho Chi Minh's trust / Lost on the behind

Blondie

"Heart of Glass"

Mucho mistrust / Love's gone behind

We're never gonna survive homelessness, we get a little crazy

Seal

"Crazy"   5:53

We're never gonna survive unless we get a little crazy

Now the oboe may be there to greet them

Now the old boy may be barely breathing

Singing songs about the subway

Lynyrd Skynyrd
"Sweet Home Alabama" 4:43

Singing songs about the South lands

I tickle Lulu while we're looking for Mookie

Van Halen
"Everybody Wants Some!!" 3:59

I take a mobile line looking for a moonbeam

You've got a fart so big, it could crush this town

Tom Petty
"Walls" 4:24

You've got a heart so big, it could crush this town

Oh, we are sailing, yes, give Jesus pants

John Lennon and the Plastic Ono Band
"Give Peace a Chance" 4:50

All we are saying is "Give peace a chance"

She'll have fun, fun, fun, 'til Daddy takes the tea bag away

The Beach Boys

"Fun, Fun, Fun" 2:18

. . . 'til Daddy takes the T-Bird away

She was two-timing naked / He was too tired to fight about it

---

The Eagles

"Life in the Fast Lane"

She was too tired to make it / He was too tired to fight about it

My country steals from me

Traditional

"My Country 'Tis of Thee"

My country, 'tis of thee

No matter what your french fries tell you, we were made to fall in love

---

Bobby Brown

"Every Little Step" 3:59

No matter what your friends try to tell you, we were made to fall in love

Ham on rye

Kenny Loggins
"I'm Alright" 3:53

I'm alright

Pay the rent collect

Prince
"Little Red Corvette" 4:58

Little red Corvette

All I wanna do is lick a sick ox

Spice Girls

"Wannabe"

 2:52

All I wanna do is zig-uh-zig-ah!

I'm not colored crap

Nirvana

"Lithium"

3:14

I'm not gonna crack

Here he comes, that scab-faced clown

The Everly Brothers

"Cathy's Clown" 2:25

Here he comes, that's Cathy's clown

Why do I find it so hard to write the next line? /
'Cause I've got no ink in my pen

Spandau Ballet
"True"

5:41

*Why do I find it so hard to write the next line? /
Oh, I want the truth to be said*

Do it in the ditch!

Salt-N-Pepa

"Push It"

Get up on this!

Oh, oat bran, he can't help it when his hubby
looks insane

Pearl Jam

"Even Flow"

---

*Oh, dark grin, he can't help, when he's happy
looks insane*

I was with a kangaroo in a railway station

Brewer and Shipley
"One Toke Over the Line" 3:17

Sitting downtown in a railway station

An evil mass of jelly calling you back

No Doubt

"Spiderwebs"

Leave a message and I'll call you back

And zits, about twenty

The B-52's

"Love Shack"

It sits about twenty

Does she miss you, existing just to kiss you, like the one-eyed girl?

Melissa Etheridge

"Like the Way I Do"

. . . like the way I do?

Well, lift us up, we'll weed the lawn

Joe Cocker and Jennifer Warnes

"Up Where We Belong" *4:00*

Love lifts us up where we belong

- I'm such a baby, the doormat makes me cry
- I'm such a baby, the doorbell makes me cry
- I'm such a baby, the darkness makes me cry

Hootie and the Blowfish

"Only Wanna Be With You"

I'm such a baby 'cause the Dolphins make me cry

Ma's ain't the kind of place to raise your kids

Elton John

"Rocket Man"

Mars ain't the kind of place to raise your kids

Poor son, shoot your own leg

Def Leppard

"Pour Some Sugar on Me"

Pour some sugar on me

One Mormon dance with you in the moonlight

Van Morrison

"Moondance" 4:30

One more moondance with you in the moonlight

Every girl's crazy for a shotglass man

ZZ Top

"Sharp Dressed Man" 4:13

Every girl's crazy for a sharp-dressed man

Cycle killer, Custer says

Talking Heads
"Psycho Killer" *3:57*

Psycho killer, qu'est-que c'est?

I can feel my body rot

Taylor Dayne
"Tell It to My Heart" 4:00

I can feel my body rock

Now I'm staring at papayas as they dance across
the floor

Greg Kihn 2:50

"The Break-Up Song (They Don't Write 'Em)"

---

*Now I'm staring at their bodies as they dance
across the floor*

The sky's in love with you

Herb Alpert

"This Guy's in Love with You" *3:58*

This guy's in love with you

You better shape up before you pee the bed

John Travolta and Olivia Newton-John

"You're the One That I Want"

You better shape up, 'cause I need a man

To leave you there by yourself chained to plates

Live
"I Alone" 3:38

To leave you there by yourself, chained to fate

- Gonna use my sausage
- Gonna use my soft-sell
- Gonna use my senses
- Gonna use my salt cell
- Gonna use my saute
- Gonna use my sassy

The Pretenders

"Brass in Pocket"

Gonna use my sidestep

I've got my man scent on you

George Harrison

"Got My Mind Set on You"

I've got my mind set on you

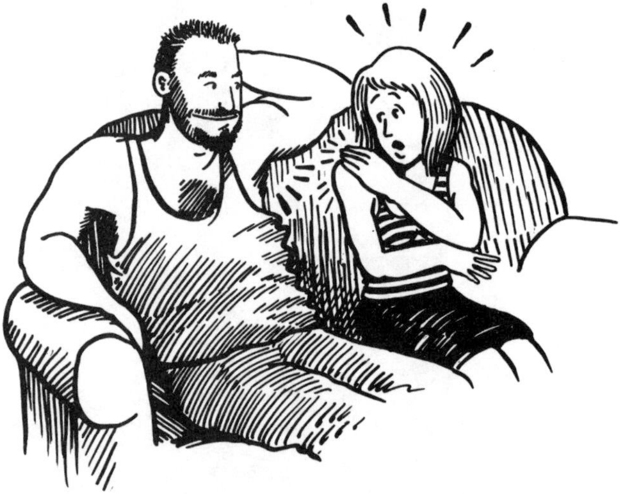

A death-row hard-on two minutes too late

Alanis Morissette
"Ironic" 3:50

A death-row pardon two minutes too late

I am a dump truck / I am a dump truck

Living Colour
"Cult of Personality"

I am the cult of / I am the cult of

Are we gonna let the alligator bring us down?

Prince and the Revolution
"Let's Go Crazy" 4:39

R we gonna let de-elevator bring us down?

When I'm tired of taking coke / I hide in my music

Boston

"More Than a Feeling"

When I'm tired and thinking cold / I hide in my music

- My sweet Georgia
- My eyes were torture

Frankie Valli

"My Eyes Adored You" 3:25

My eyes adored you

I know that the hippie ties never lie

The Who

"Won't Get Fooled Again" 8:34

I know that the hypnotized never lie

Stood there bowling, sweating in the sun

Bob Seger

"Like a Rock" 5:56

Stood there boldly, sweating in the sun

I got ten-ton pebbles and a microphone

Beck
"Where It's At" 5:25

I got two turntables and a microphone

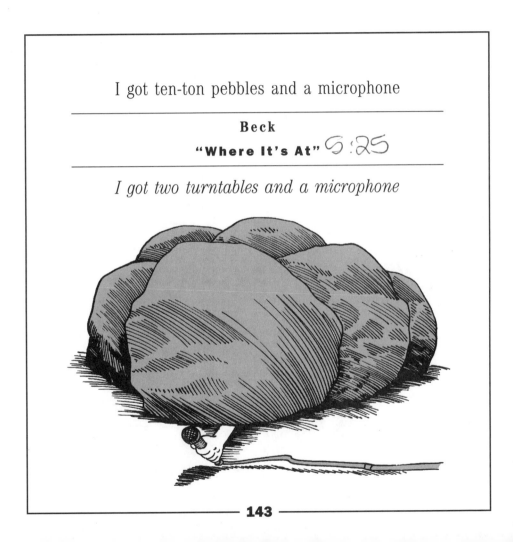

- Lunatic friends
- Women take French

"Lunatic Fringe"

Lunatic fringe

I have spoke with a ton of angels

U2 4:38

"I Still Haven't Found What I'm Looking For"

I have spoke in the tongue of angels

Windshield wipers, turpentine

Janis Joplin

"Me and Bobby McGee" 4:33

Windshield wipers slappin' time

- Permanent mustache
- Oreo big stuff, uh-huh
- Call the Coast Guard, uh-huh

The Ohio Players
"Love Rollercoaster" 4:43

Love rollercoaster

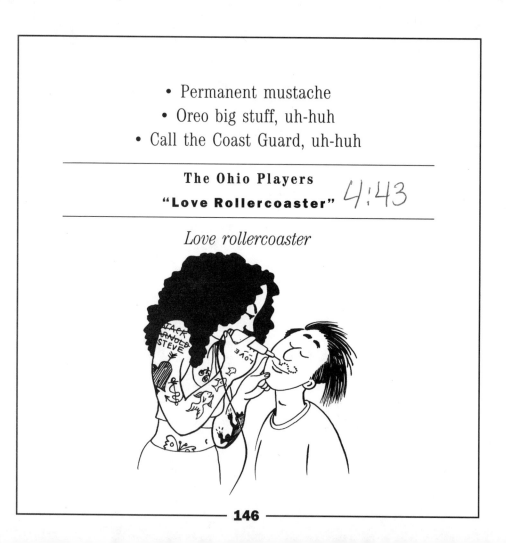

She got the big kablooies, Cherry Cherry

Neil Diamond

"Cherry Cherry" *2:30*

She got the way to move me, Cherry Cherry

The passions that collide in me / While my man's
inside of me

Sheena Easton

"For Your Eyes Only" *3:08*

---

*The passions that collide in me / The wild,
abandoned side of me*

Wish that I were a fat-free crane, jumping, juggling
on down to New Orleans

Creedence Clearwater Revival

"Born on the Bayou" 5:08

---

*Wish that I were a fast freight train, just
a-joogling on down to New Orleans*

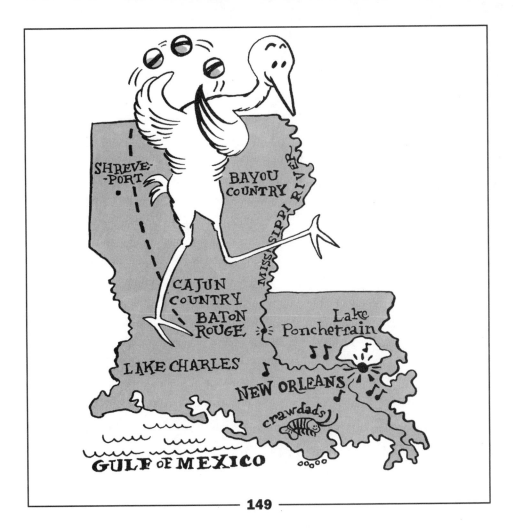

Jesus is just a rat with beads

The Doobie Brothers
"Jesus Is Just Alright" 4:20

Jesus is just alright with me

We were cool on Christ

Wang Chung
"Dance Hall Days" 4:14

We were cool and crazed

Those dirty witch clothes even fit me

The Clash 3:18

"Should I Stay or Should I Go?"

Don't you know which clothes even fit me?

- Got a mushy head
- Got a moshing head

Bush

"Machinehead" 4:29

Got a machinehead

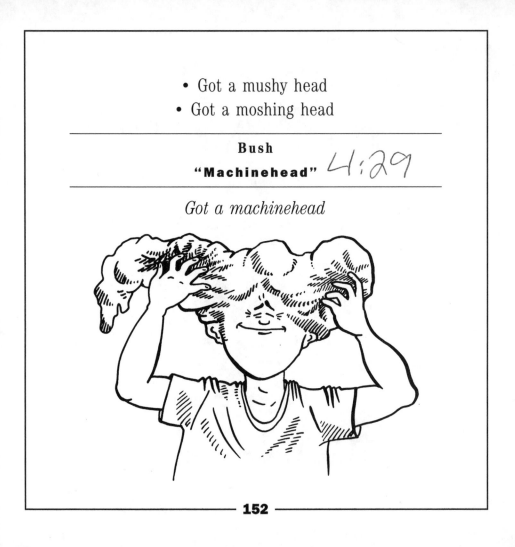

Something inside has tied a napkin tight

Carole King

"It's Too Late" *3:53*

Something inside has died and I can't hide

I'm blowing a penguin / I'm down on my knees

Green Day

"Geek Stink Breath" *3:00*

I'm blowing off steam with methamphetamine

If there's a busload in your headshow, don't be a
lawman

Led Zeppelin

"Stairway to Heaven"

---

*If there's a bustle in your hedgerow, don't be
alarmed now*

I'll pretend my shit's not stinking

Go West

"King of Wishful Thinking" 4:06

I'll pretend my ship's not sinking

Summertime, and the women is easy

Sarah Vaughn
"Summertime"

Summertime, and the livin' is easy

Beavis says you're freaky and everybody's shaky, but we're stayin' alive

---

The Bee Gees

"Stayin' Alive"

Feel the city breakin' and everybody's shakin', and we're stayin' alive

Then you flew your liver down to Nova Scotia

Carly Simon

"You're So Vain"

Then you flew your Learjet down to Nova Scotia

Double in size

INXS
"Devil Inside" 5:10

Devil inside

157

Crap shooter, how come you taste so good?

 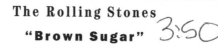

Brown sugar, how come you taste so good?

I was on the Muppets

Nine Inch Nails

"Down in It"

I was up above it

Pair of dice by the dashboard light

Meat Loaf 8:29

"Paradise by the Dashboard Light"

Paradise by the dashboard light

Lost in the ocean

Lisa Lisa and Cult Jam with Full Force

"Lost in Emotion" 5:03

Lost in emotion

Can I get some lemonade?

The Black Crowes
"Remedy" 4:50

Can I get a remedy?

I started school in a worn, torn dress and
somebody threw up

The Supremes
"Love Child" *2:58*

---

*I started school in a worn, torn dress that
somebody threw out*

No one wants to beat the fetus

Michael Jackson
"Beat It" *4:16*

No one wants to be defeated

Lord, I was born an M&M

The Allman Brothers Band
"Ramblin' Man"

4:48

Lord, I was born a ramblin' man

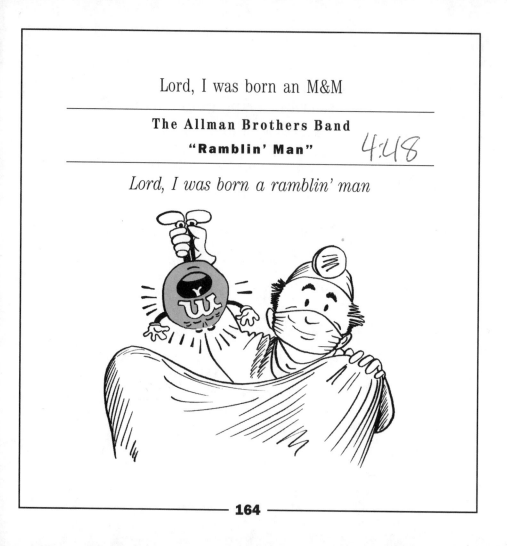

- Cramps my gut, baby we were born to run
- Tracks like dust, baby we were born to run

Bruce Springsteen

"Born to Run" 5:30

Tramps like us, baby we were born to run

Who needs a house out of hackeysacks?

Billy Joel

"Movin' Out (Anthony's Song)"

Who needs a house out in Hackensack?

- Back to the howling gold out in the woods
  - Back to the habitat out in the woods
  - Back to the hello—no, out in the woods

Elton John

"Goodbye Yellow Brick Road"

Back to the howling old owl in the woods

We could gather, throw up beer

R.E.M.

"Sitting Still"

We could gather, throw a fit

Eatin' walrus skin

Steve Winwood
"Freedom Overspill" 5:30

Freedom overspill

I sleep around

The Foo Fighters
"I'll Stick Around" 3:52

I'll stick around

And our love becomes a fuel empire

The Doors
"Light My Fire" 7:03

And our love become a funeral pyre

Voyeurs in love

Jackson Browne
"Lawyers in Love" 4:30

Lawyers in love

On a dark desert highway, Cool Whip in my hair

The Eagles

"Hotel California"

On a dark desert highway, cool wind in my hair

One of us here has smelly feet

James Taylor

"Your Smiling Face"

Whenever I see your smiling face

Grab my chicken bone

Nirvana

"Sliver"

Grandma take me home

Shoot the children with no shoes on their feet

The Steve Miller Band

"Fly Like an Eagle" 4:48

Shoe the children with no shoes on their feet

- Tried to give you constellations
- Tried to give you constipation

Derek and the Dominoes

"Layla" 7:05

Tried to give you consolation

Thunder rollin', can't go swimmin', it's rainin'

Fleetwood Mac

"Dreams" 4:14

Thunder only happens when it's rainin'

Went to a dance, looking for a man

The Beach Boys

"Barbara Ann" 2:52

Went to a dance, looking for romance

Isn't he a bitch like you and me?

The Beatles
"Nowhere Man" *2:45*

Isn't he a bit like you and me?

So let us not talk falsely now, but I was getting
laid

Jimi Hendrix

"All Along the Watchtower"

---

*So let us not talk falsely now, for the hour is
getting late*

Everyone needs a panda who loves you

John Cougar
"Hand to Hold on to" 3:30

Everyone needs a hand to hold on to

You can dance, for respiration

You can dance, for inspiration

You got the beet juice, I got the beets

Def Leppard

"Pour Some Sugar on Me"

You got the peaches, I got the cream

She's alone in the neutral ocean

Beck

"The New Pollution" 3:43

She's in love with the new pollution

That's what I said: "Amen, nice shirt"

Filter

"Hey Man, Nice Shot"

That's why I say, "Hey man, nice shot"

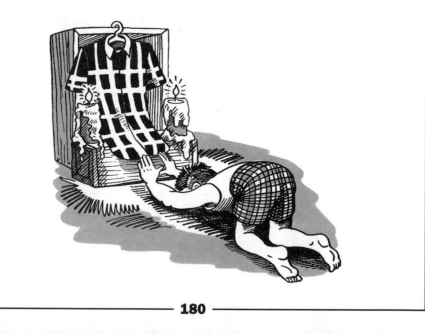

Acknowledgements

Since these three volumes of mondegreens are now approaching a total of a thousand misheard lyrics, to admit that many of these songs were mangled by other people is just another way of saying that I'm sane and can carry on an everyday conversation. Thousands of people have shared their mistakes with me—or culled the errors of friends—and I appreciate every single letter. I am especially grateful to the following people, who sent me the mondegreens that appear in this book:

Amber Allen, Mercedes Allen, Peg Allen, Dave Andrew, Eric Andrews, Krista Austin, M. Baird, Viki Bankey, Michael Bergen, the Bernbaums, William R. Bitters, Amy Boeck, Gretchen Boyd, John C. Bradley, Jamie K. Branson, Jay Brewer, Andy Brill, Daniel Brotschul, Eleanor M. Brown, Sharon and Bruce Brown, Tracy Brzychi, Mary Burke, Desiree Cagle, L. Tyler Cain, Joanna Caldwell, Emily Callahan, Jason Calsyn, Sharon J. Cardellicchio, Norman L. Carlos, Jennifer Carpenter and Lauren-Alice Lamanna, Jim Carriglio, Carlos Castells-Hogan, Vivian Castengera, Maria E. Causey, James C. Chetrick, Marcia Chicca, Alexander Chisholm, Jake

Christiansen, Rebecca L. Clark, Lynn Anne Cochran, Carol Cook, Tom Cooper, Sean Coughlin, Leah Culligan, Rivers Cuomo, Keely Daniel, R. D'Apice, Amy Davis, Skye Davis, Keith R. P. Dickens, Jamie and Bill Doebler, Michael J. Donlon, Tracey Dorame, Lisa Drillis, Jennifer Drissen, Al Duque, Rebecca Esparza, Anna-Lisa Espinoza, Kathryn Faulkner, Chris Fishel, Bob Fisher, Betsy Foss, Daniela Friedman, Roxane R. Fritz, Stan Fujishin, Stephanie Gagnon, Claudine Gandolfi, Becky Gardner, Lori M. Gargas, Donna Garlock, Jamie Ghione, Mary Laura Gibbs, Rachel Glass, Judi Goldfarb, Lisa Goldstein, Alex E. Gonzalez, Logan Graves, Alexis and Lance Grucela, Adrienne Hagen, Alex Hamberg, Allison Hart, Laurie Hayes, Christina Heldreth, Larry Hennessey, Meghan Herz, Aimee J. Hickman, Julie Hock, Liz Hogan, Bruce Hoo, Laska E. R. Hook, Dan Howlett, Pam Hunt, Siobhan Hyde, Christie Ingenito, Larry Jenkins, Paula R. Kalafarski, Alison Kavey, Bridget Keenan, Ann Kennedy, the Ketts, Mark Kieler, Mark Tapio Kines, John C. Kirkpatrick, the Klausners, Babs Klein, Istvan Kobzos, Robert and Jessica Koenig, Gary S. Koshi, Jeane C. Kropp, Yelena and Erica Krug, Robert Lagomarsino, Kristie Lamm, Rebecca Lane, Chris Lee, Bridget LeRoy, Charlene D. Lipkus, Rene A. Louviere Jr., Sheryl L. Loyce, Jimmy Luth, Alicia Mackenthun, Richard Madow, Steven McElroy, Jeffrey P. McManus, E. McReynolds, Pete Meriwether, Elizabeth L. Micciche, McKenzie Milanowski, Hasmin and David Miller, Leigh Miller, Karen Millett, Kay Moffett, Mitch Moore, Elaine Mossman, Susan Mudgett, Dion Navarro, Gary Negbaur, Fred Nelson, Isaac Nelson, Bruce W. Niedt, Steven Nogaj, Brenda Nopper, Emily Nussbaum, Jobi and Jordana Okin,

Kim Owens, Susan Pecoraro, J.R. Pella, Jeannine Poole, Jill Portugal, Lynn Presley, Michelle Primeau, Elizabeth Pulver, John Raab, Anne Rieman, Paul J. Roberts, Mark S. Robreau, Gabe Romano, Pattie Rothstein, Cara Rucinski, Martin Russell, Sammy Sammon, Riita Santala, Kim H. Saretsky, Dava Schilder, James J. Schweitzer, Dave Schwind, Michele Semenec, Lisa Simms, Stacey Skillern, Allen Smalling, Barbara and George Smead, Erika Smith, Virginia Smith, Jennie Spinner, Carrie Sprague, Devon and Gordon Sproule, Betty J. Stafford, Jason Stanley, Darren Stansbury, Dean Starnes, Sandi Lee Strot, Julie Sutton, Christy Sylvester and Rebecca Howell, Michael Taylor, John Terra, Caitlin Tierney, Eve Tolpa, Anita Tucker, Christine L. Tuohy, Maggie Vaisman, Sarah Walrand, Karen Ward, Sherry Waters, Bill Weinberg, Benjamin Weiner, Karen L. Weis, Natalie Welsh, Barbara S. Whitlock, Marty Whitt, Michael Will, Chris Wilson, Andy Wyke, Sam Yoder, Cindy Yogmas, Dan Zalewski, and Stephanie Ziobro.

If you have misheard lyrics of your own (or of a friend!) that you'd like to pass along, please send them to me, Gavin Edwards, at P.O. Box 023291, Brooklyn, NY 11202-3291. Mondegreens of any genre are welcome: country classics, Irish drinking songs, and especially Christmas carols. But hurry—as ever, I can acknowledge only the first person to send me each misheard lyric.

My deepest thanks to Shary Flenniken, both for her fabulous illustrations in this book and for being a cool person in general. If you enjoyed her art here, go find some of her "Trots and Bonnie" strips in old issues of *National Lampoon,* or failing that, check out her "Wet Dreams" collector cards. (Don't write outraged letters about the smut quotient—they're illustrations of dreams about water.) For a twelve-card set, send $5 to Starhead Comics, P.O. Box 30044, Seattle WA 98103, and mention this book.

I am grateful to this book's editor, Dan Lane, for his skill and patience. And as always, I am enriched by the wit and good counsel of my marvelous agent, Gordon Kato.

I'd also like to thank Gavin Rossdale of Bush for his kindness in letting me reprint his lyrics to "Everything Zen," and Mike Pagnotta and Dave Dorrell for their aid in making it happen.

Thanks to everybody at *Details* magazine, especially Joe Levy, who is not just my editor but a friend and a mensch.

Singling out friends and family is always a risky endeavor because of the high probability of excluding somebody, so let me just say how happy I am to be surrounded by so many good people in New York City, all across the United States and the United Kingdom, and on the Well.

Finally, I want to sing the praises of my partner in crime, Jill McManus, who brings me tasty beverages, dances with me in her pajamas, and blesses me with her presence every day of my life.

Index